TABLE OF CONENTS

PRAISES FOR "DIET DETOX"

"Diet Detox is what every woman needs to read to heal their relationship with food and their body and deepen their most important relationship: the one with their Savior! It offers encouragement, truth and practical application to help woman unravel their identity and self-worth and stop finding it in how they look."

- Taylor Kiser - Blogger at Food Faith Fitness

"Diet Detox speaks grace to the hidden shame we feel about our bodies. It breaths truth into the lies of diet culture--a culture that would have us believe we're only loveable if we look a certain way, or weigh a certain number. It's time God's children fought back against these lies, in this devotional the Body Bloved team does just that. Diet Detox accurately captures the heart of God for His children when it comes to issues of food and body image. Written by registered dietitians, each devotional is packed with scientific insight, practical advice, and spiritual truth that will help you renew your mind and transform your relationship with food. If you're sick of searching for answers in the next diet only to feel burnt out and ashamed, if you feel like God is mad at you because of your struggles with food, or that somehow you've disappointed Him with your "lack of willpower," the authors would urge you to trade your willpower for His will. And friend, His will for you is freedom. This devotional will help you find it! "

- Aubrey Golbek, RD, Author of "Grace, Food, And Everything In Between: Discover the transforming power of grace to set you free from food and body shame"

FORWARD

I had just completed a 30-day sugar fast and was feeling some food freedom, but also a little nervous about stepping back into my everyday eating patterns without the clear-cut boundaries. I was having flashbacks to the last days of my previous elimination diet attempts.

Diets are so appealing--they tell you exactly what to do (and what not to do) so you can finally feel like you're in control. That is, until you experience some life-altering upheaval like getting sick or a family member getting injured or losing a job or going through a breakup. Or simply wanting to go out and enjoy some chips and margaritas for a friend's birthday.

That's when the diet becomes a wagging finger of shame and scorn over breaking the rules.

Thankfully, that's also when I started reading Diet Detox. I knew diets felt like a revolving door of shame, but I didn't know the alarming statistics of failure rates cited in the first pages of Diet Detox.

The good thing is, Diet Detox didn't just throw a bunch of facts in my face, but revealed the true face of diet culture while reminding me that food finds its purpose in the Lord.

Cue the sigh of relief.

I know this, but reading about the Spirit-led way of eating from a variety of authors from different walks of life made me feel altogether normal, convicted, and encouraged. I felt comforted knowing I wasn't the only one struggling. I felt kindly confronted about how I was letting food take the place of Christ. I felt encouraged that I could (not "should") make new choices each day, and therefore looked forward to each new day of reading.

Being a mom of two littles, a personal trainer, and author, I need to spend my time wisely. I can honestly say Diet Detox was a devotional that was both doable and effective. I could set aside a few minutes to read it every morning, and not only was it easy to digest but deeply soul-nourishing with the concise teaching and prayer at the end.

If you have ever felt the weight of trying to figure out food and failing, or just need a gentle reminder that the kingdom of God is not about eating and drinking, but of righteousness, peace, and joy in the Holy Spirit, I would recommend Diet Detox. I'm confident you'll look forward to each day of this 30-day journey as a way to reset your sight on the Lord, to renew your thanksgiving for His daily bread, and to grow stronger in grace.

With gratitude,

Kasey Shuler, Author of "Move for Joy: An Intuitive Training Approach to Pursue God in Fitness and Find Happiness"

A NOTE FROM THE AUTHORS

It's time to lay down your diet shakes, cleanses and detoxes.
Just lay them right on down…at the foot of the cross.
Whatever you're counting – calories, grams, points, steps,
macros – you have our permission to stop, quit striving, rest,
and re-evaluate.

It's exhausting, isn't it? And here's the thing – dieting to lose
weight may not be doing anything to improve your health in
the long run.

Dieting might give you a sense of feeling in control –
controlling every morsel you put in your mouth, controlling
the numbers on the scale, controlling calories in with calories
out – but it's all an illusion. It might seem like you have
control over your body and your weight, but researchers have
found that 80-90% of people who lose weight gain it back, and
many tack on a few extra pounds from where they first
started. In fact, dieting is actually associated with weight gain,
not weight loss! Dieters gain a few other things too – a
sluggish metabolism, a low self-esteem, and stress concerning
eating and exercise.

Beloved, there's only One in control, and He's inviting you to
let Him take back the reigns, to move over and let Him drive.
He wants to drive you down a path of freedom from food
struggles. He wants you to stop striving to be less…or more
and start striving to know Him.

We know your weight concerns feel…well…weighty. If you could just lose a few pounds…then all of your problems will be solved. Right? You could start really living. This devotional is an invitation to stop striving, to stop counting, to stop detoxing, and to start living now. Right now. As you are. In the body He gave you.

Your body feels imperfect, we get it. Instead of trying to change your body, consider changing how you think about your body. It's the world's ways that make us feel imperfect.

In Romans 12:2, we're reminded,

> Do not conform to the pattern of this world, but be transformed by the renewing of your mind. Then you will be able to test and approve what God's will is – his good, pleasing and perfect will.

The world tells us what is beautiful and loveable. It's time we looked to our Heavenly Father to tell us that.

You might have picked this little book up because you thought it was a diet book – a devotional full of dieting inspiration. A way to get back on track. Your very last diet kick-in-the-pants. The one that will finally work. Well, Beloved, sorry to say, the book you picked up is exactly the opposite of a diet. Read the title again. This book isn't a detox diet. It's a diet detox.

A detox from our culture that says we have to be a certain dress size to be loveable.

A detox from the belief that thin = beautiful.

A detox from the pursuit of weight loss and dieting that takes the pleasure right out of mealtime.

A detox from miserable exercise routines in the name of weight loss and abs.

Our hope is that you'll run from dieting and the need for six pack abs with full "ab-andon" and run into the arms of the One who made you and loves you just as you are.

This little devotional was written by a team of folks – married, single, stay-at-home parents, working parents, health care professionals, but most importantly children of God. We all care about the same thing – helping others heal in their relationship with food and fully embrace their unique bodies, which were meant to be different shapes and sizes. We believe that every body is a good body!

We deeply care about your health and well-being. We are all for balanced meals and enjoyable forms of physical activity. We also believe that food should be a source of pleasure. Food brings people together, creating fellowship and connection. Food is meant to be celebrated, savored, and enjoyed. God gave us a wide variety of food options to make the eating experience pleasurable and nourishing. He made our bodies in such a way that they function best with a wide variety of colors, textures, and flavors.

Food matters.
However, as a culture, it seems we've all taken food concerns a bit too far. We're seeing a diet-crazed, thin-obsessed culture that's headed down a dark path. We wrote this book in an effort to redirect our brothers and sisters in Christ down a healthier, more fulfilling path. We felt God's gentle nudge to write this book so that worrisome thoughts over food can be replaced with thoughts of self-love, love for others, and love for Jesus.

Our hope for you is that through this daily devotional, you will find the courage to stop stressing about food and start putting it back into its place as just one minor piece of your life. We pray for complete healing from struggles surrounding food, exercise and body image. Jesus came so that peace and love would reign over war and hate. As a culture, we are at war with our bodies. We declare body peace to reign over body hate.

To do our part, we've weaved together scriptures, words of encouragement, analogies, and prayers to shine a light on a counter-cultural message that we believe will bring health, wholeness, and healing to Christian communities.

We have prayed for you, dear reader, before your journey even began. In His name, we prayed that you would be astounded by His everlasting love for you and that you would have the courage to walk away from dieting forever, and find your way to healing and wholeness.

B. Loved. B. Accepted. B. Free

With love,

The Body Bloved Team

DIET DETOX

30 Day Devotional
to Ditching Diets and Claiming Christ's Love

BODY BLOVED

GOODBYE DIETS

DAY 1: PINKY PROMISE?

Promises of weight loss flood our media, from infomercials, to the next best weight loss plan, to magazine covers promising to rid you of your belly fat. Doctors, nurses, dietitians, and even hypnotists are making promises on their seemingly legitimate websites that they can help you lose weight. They're making promises…promises they can't keep.

Nine out of ten people who lose weight regain it. Yes, that's the cold hard truth. That doesn't keep people from trying! Everyone believes they will magically be the one person who doesn't gain it back. The odds are slim.

In fact, not a single study of a single weight loss program has EVER shown that the *majority* of participants lost weight and kept the weight off. EVER. And it's not for a lack of trying. There have been literally thousands of weight loss clinical trials. Not one has ever worked.

And the reason scientists haven't cracked this code is because our bodies are actually designed to survive the periods of famine and starvation our ancestors endured for human survival. So your body's fight to hold onto the weight is actually an amazing gift from our Heavenly Father to keep us alive!

The dieting industry promised that if you just tried hard enough, you'd be thin. They promised 20 pounds by summer. They promised the weight would drop from your belly or your thighs. They promised. And if they were there standing right in front of you, they probably would have pinky promised.

But, they couldn't keep their promise.

It's time we wave our white flags and surrender. And while we're at it, let's get on our knees and surrender to the One who made us in His image. Our Heavenly Father gave us the perfect gift in making our bodies robust and sturdy, even durable.

Beloved, it's time to shift your focus from broken promises of the diet industry to that one promise that can never be broken – God's unwavering love. He will love you unconditionally just as you are, in all your glory, and brokenness, fat or thin.

In Isaiah 54:10, God says,

> *Though the mountains be shaken and the hills be removed, yet my unfailing love for you will not be shaken nor my covenant of peace be removed," says the LORD, who has compassion on you.*

God's love is one pinky promise that can't be broken. May we rest in that promise today.

Dear God, we praise you for your promise to love us unconditionally. We accept that love from you. Protect us from the false promises from others and show us Your truths instead. Amen.

DAY 2: AMERICAN IDOLS

Idols aren't just Hollywood superstars. They are people and things that we center our lives around, or run after. According to Webster's dictionary, an idol is "a representation or symbol of an object of worship or a false God." An idol is something that we pursue because we believe it will solve our problems and fix our deepest longings and needs.

Idols are tricky because they often start off as innocent desires that are justified as being necessary for health and happiness. Money, a good job, healthy lifestyle patterns – these are all good things. However, we're easily seduced into believing that these earthly pursuits must take center stage, and that's when they become idols.

How do you know if pursuing a healthy lifestyle has become an idol? Here's one way to find out – ask yourself how much time you spend thinking about food, exercise, and/or the way your body looks in comparison to how much time you spend thinking about the One true King, Jesus Christ? Drop the mic!

When our hope is in achieving the perfect body through the perfect diet, then our hope has been misdirected. When our heart and mind feel paralyzed or condemned by concern over food choices, then dieting has teetered across the line to idol worship. This type of idolatry screams lies of shame rather than speaking the truth of our hope in Jesus.

See, this is the problem with dieting – it takes a lot of mental and physical energy to keep track of foods, exercise regimens, and numbers on the scale. So much energy, in fact, these diets often become idols.

Worries about calories, portions, step-counters clutter our minds, taking us away from THE ONE who can bring us freedom - Jesus Christ. He wants you to be free from obsessive thoughts about food and your body because He is a jealous God who wants your full attention.

As the Psalmist states in 25:5,

> *Lead me by your truth and teach me, for you are the God who saves me. All day long I put my hope in you.*

Is the dieting rollercoaster keeping you in bondage? If so, you're not alone. Researchers have studied thousands of dieters over the years and discovered three common themes. First, diets don't work. People lose weight at first but most gain it back in the long run. Second, dieting is associated with eating disorders. In fact, just about every individual who has struggled with an eating disorder will tell you that it all started with an innocent diet. Third, researchers have found that dieting has negative effects on emotional well-being. Of course it does! Dieting takes us away from experiencing the peace that passes all understanding that we get directly from God.

Dear God, thank You for your invitation to seek healing in our relationship with food and our bodies and to break free from the bondage of idols such as diets. Open our eyes to Your truth and calm the battles in the mind that speak lies about our bodies and what we eat.

DAY 3: KNOWN

We all long to be known. We can trace this longing back as far as Adam in the garden of Eden when he longed for a companion who would be like him, who would know him. It is an instinct, a need, deep within us that has existed since the beginning of time.

Almost more than the need to know another person, we desire to be known, to have someone see who we really are, see into the complexity and hidden places of our heart, see into the hopes and dreams of who we are becoming. We long for someone to know intimately and love us despite our flaws and failures, short comings and inadequacies.

Without God, we try to fill this need with a spouse, children, friends, sex, money, pleasure, health, a better diet and lifestyle, a life of doing good for others, a larger following on social media...all of which are good in and of themselves, but they can never satisfy this God-sized hole and they will ultimately leave us empty.

But God.

Born of a virgin in human flesh, He came to earth to be our Emmanuel – God With Us. He came to know us, to experience what we experience, to feel what we feel, to be the perfect High Priest who is able to sympathize with our weaknesses and overcome temptation, sin, and even death itself (Hebrews 4:15).
Beloved, you are known by God. Galatians 4:9a reads,

But now that you have come to know God, or rather to be known by God, how can you turn back again to the weak and worthless elementary principles of the world?

It's often tempting to try to change our bodies in an effort to be noticed, to be known. The world tells us this is necessary. God tells us it isn't.

We *can* be known and *are* known by a living, holy God who loves us and has adopted us as children, heirs to His unsearchable riches. What a glorious truth! How often do we take this precious knowledge for granted and turn again to the glittering distractions of this world! May God help us keep our eyes always on the One who knows us and gave Himself for us.

Dear Lord, thank you for knowing each of us. We ask that you fill up our God-sized hole with your presence as we seek to turn away from the unsatisfying ways of the world. Amen.

DAY 4: WIND CHASING

Have you ever seen a dog chase it's tail? Spinning around and around, working so hard to grasp it. He is often unsuccessful at catching it, but every so often there is that dog that manages it. He grabs it for a moment, victorious! A fleeting moment of gratification, relief from the hard work, and then he has to release his tail and bid it adieu until the next round of chase.

Tail-chasing sounds like dieting, doesn't it?

A new diet begins with a certain weight or clothing size goal. Hard work is put in. We start out each day in an effort to be "good" with eating. We navigate the food landmines in our paths – donuts at the office, treats at bible study, bread before dinner, fit in the exercise to balance out what we eat, and then cross the finish line when we crawl into bed at night. We wake up the next day, rinse and repeat.

Sometimes the weight or size goal is grasped, but usually it is a fleeting moment of gratification, followed by relief from the hard work, and then the diet is released, because researchers have found that the weight creeps back on for most people. So, we bid the diet adieu until the next round of chase commences.

We are chasing an image of what we think our body should look like. But what are we really chasing? Satisfaction? Contentment? Happiness? We believe that if we look a certain way, that these things will be ours. "If I can just be size X, if I can just weigh X pounds, I know I will be happy and feel so much better."

And so we toil and chase contentment.

Ecclesiastes 4:4 says,
> And I saw that all labor and all achievement spring from
> man's envy of his neighbor. This too is meaningless, a
> chasing after the wind.

The wind - joy, peace, satisfaction, wholeness apart from God
– it just can't be caught. We want happiness, we envy and
want to look like the women we see in magazines and on TV.
We think we want what they have. And around every corner
we are sold a diet that promises to get us there.

But all this is meaningless, a chasing after the wind.

These things can only be found in God.

Beloved, what if we stopped chasing the wind and rested in
God instead?

*Lord, thank you that you see me and love me the way that I am right
at this moment. I pray that instead of chasing after the wind that I
rest in you. Please help me build my trust that joy and contentment
comes from you and you alone. Amen.*

DAY 5: GOODBYE OLD SELF

Finding peace in your relationship with food is a journey. The first step on this journey is a scary one. It involves walking away from the dieting mindset. Walking away from a lifelong hobby of dieting requires a complete leap of faith – a commitment to stop counting calories and instead to listen to your body's cues and cravings.

The dieting mindset isn't serving you well. Counting calories, restricting, and guilting yourself to the gym isn't leading to a life of freedom, and it may even be getting in the way of your walk with the Lord.

It might be time to strip off the old dieting self so that you can put on the new non-dieting self in its place. The apostle Paul spoke of this old self/new self concept in Ephesians 4:22-24. While he wasn't specifically talking about dieting, his words of wisdom still apply:

> *You were taught to put away your former way of life, your old self, corrupt and deluded by its lusts, and to be renewed in the spirit of your minds, and to clothe yourselves with the new self, created according to the likeness of God in true righteousness and holiness.*

Paul says the former self is "deluded by its lusts." As a culture, we've been deluded by the media to believe that beauty and health must look a certain way. He challenges us to clothe ourselves with the new self, which is less like culture and more like God. We cannot live into our new self without shedding ourselves of the old mindset.

Beloved, are you lusting after the wrong things? Strip off that old dieting self. Perhaps today is the day to throw that scale in the trashcan, or donate those old, old, clothes that don't fit to your local thrift shop.

Put on the new non-dieting self – the self that doesn't stress about food and instead celebrates and savors a wide variety of flavors, colors, and textures; a self that is "created according to the likeness of God." Then run free towards wholeness and healing in your relationship with food, fitness and your body.

Dear God, give us the courage to walk away from dieting forever and never look back. Help us to notice those old dieting thoughts that creep up from time-to-time and to replace them with thoughts of you and your unconditional love for us. Quiet the desire for thinness and set up little reminders in our lives that a life spent in dieting bondage is not a full and abundant life. Amen.

DAY 6: A DIETER'S REPENTANCE

Some of us are terrible with directions and therefore become U-turn pros. "Whoops, missed that turn." "Ugh! That was the street I wanted!" "Ack, was it *that* freeway exit?!"

GPS might have sent you down a path in the pursuit of physical health. Maybe it was a visit to the doctor, or an inspiring documentary that sparked an interest in changing up your routine. Attempts at being more physically active and eating more balanced meals might have started out in the right direction, but it's also possible you missed a turn somewhere. And now you're headed down a slippery dieting slope that has you anxious about each and every bite. Well, it just might be time to make a U-turn.

Repentance can be a scary word. It doesn't need to be. It just means that we have been going in the wrong direction somehow. Perhaps you have never thought about repentance in the context of dieting, but think about it. The dieting mind-set can be hard to give up and some of us might have to go through a repentance process with the Lord in order to change course.

This means coming to a place where we are willing to admit that there might have been times we put our dieting goals, counting calories, or beating away at our bodies for the sake of worldly success front and center. This realization might bring us to our knees.

There are two pieces to repentance. First, there's turning away FROM. We turn away from the dieting mind-set of putting food rules on a pedestal over following God's heart for us and His people. Second, there's a turning TOWARDS. We turn towards the Lord for direction and healing. Hosea 6:1 says,

Come, let us return to the Lord; for it is he who has torn, and he will heal us; he has struck down, and he will bind us up.

God will heal us when we return to Him after a season of wandering around the dry desert of dieting. Turning away from worries over food and body is not an easy journey and it requires a change in mind-set.

Minds must change from striving to be "good" to earn God's approval to a mind-set that we are *already* loved. You are fully and completely loved just how your body is right now. You are loved regardless of your food choices or sloth-like patterns.

Our mind-set must be shifted from self-loathing to self-love because these lovely thoughts are the way God views us. Today, we turn towards our loving Father and ask Him to show us the path out of dieting bondage and towards gentle self-care that glorifies and honors him.

Dear loving Father, we confess that we've often put other earthly desires before you. We've been led to believe that controlling food, exercising more and pursuing a certain look is a worthy use of our time and energy. Now we realize we've taken a wrong turn. Give us the courage to turn away from those patterns and guide us in a new direction that leads to physical, emotional, and spiritual healing and self-love. Amen.

DAY 7: LAY IT DOWN

Are you tired? Tired of obsessing about what you just ate, or didn't eat or that you didn't exercise yesterday? Lay it down. It's dragging you down; it's getting in the way. Sin clings very tightly and when you're fixated on your body, food or your next workout, you might miss out on the good things that God has in store.

What is God doing right now in your life? Maybe He has a neighbor in mind who could use a little TLC, or a co-worker He'd like you to befriend. He may even be calling you to volunteer with a local organization, pursue a new career, or return home to take care of a loved one. He has big plans for you. Plans that will not only shape and mold you into becoming more Christ-like, but also plans that will let you shine His light into the world.

He longs to show you the way, to give you little nudges towards the plans He has made.
There's no space for distractions. Fixate on Him alone. God wants to use you just as you are. He's not waiting for you to be thinner, buffer, or more flexible. He's ready to use you right now.

In Hebrews we are reminded that we must first lay aside our sin before we can follow after God's plan.

> *Therefore, since we are surrounded by so great a cloud of witnesses, let us also lay aside every weight, and sin which clings so closely, and let us run with endurance the race that is set before us. - Hebrews 12:1*

29

Walking around with sin is like walking around with a ball and chain that keeps you from running your race freely. What is the sin that's holding you back? Is it obsessing over the scale, or stressing out in the aisles of the grocery store over ingredients and food labels?

Or maybe your sin looks more sloth-like with bags of potato chips on the couch and three seasons of your favorite show to catch up on. Sin takes many forms and yet all sin has one things in common - it keeps us distracted from the One who wants to show us the way.

Dear Lord, we come to you and lay our sin at Your feet. You know what that is for each of us and thank you for loving us unconditionally. We pray for the courage to step away from the fixations that plague us and distract us from your plans for our lives. We look with expectant hearts towards the path you have set for us. Amen.

BODY

DAY 8: WONDERFULLY MADE

God wasn't messing around when he made us. In fact, he was completely showing off. He created human beings - each unique, and each with built-in systems for regulation. Lungs that inflate with oxygen that travels to your tissues, a heart that pumps on its own, an immune system in place to fight infections, and a way to regulate body temperature in the coldest and hottest climates. It really is something to marvel at.

He even created systems to guide us when to eat and how much to consume. It's brilliant, really. He made it so that our stomachs expand when we eat, which sends messages to the brain signaling specific sensations of fullness. Same with hunger. We burn energy all day long, even when sitting on the couch (because it requires energy to make those lungs inflate and heart pump). And when those energy stores in our blood stream become depleted, we get another signal – hunger!

He thought of EVERYTHING! He made self-regulating bodies, complete with intricate systems of hormones, neurons, and enzymes that do their job.

The Psalmist reminds us how we are made in this famous passage (Psalm 139:14):

> *I praise you because I am fearfully and wonderfully made;*
> *your works are wonderful, I know that full well.*

Let that scripture soak in. You are fearfully and wonderfully made! As babies, we were perfectly in touch with these cues. Often as adults, we start to lose our way, and ignore the cues God gave us.

We eat when the clock says it's time, or we skip a meal when hunger strikes because of anxiety, fear, or busyness. We allow ourselves to have only a certain portion or calorie-limit despite continued feelings of physical hunger. Other times we keep eating for emotional reasons despite feeling full or because we fear never getting to enjoy that food again. We make things complicated.

God made things pretty simple.

No calorie-counting needed when you can learn to listen to your body's physical needs. Those cues are God-given and God-powered. If you feel like you have grown distant from those internal cues, there is no better time than now to practice getting back in touch with your body. Tune in to the signals He blessed you with – low energy, dizziness, irritability, hunger, contentment, fullness, overly full – all signals that can guide you in your eating decisions.

Dear Lord, we praise you for these body systems that you designed that are absolutely amazing. Remind us daily that we are truly fearfully and wonderfully made. Help us to find our way back to these hunger and fullness cues that you set in place to guide our eating decisions. Amen.

DAY 9: A LESSON IN HOSPITALITY

Some people just have that gift of hospitality. They know how to provide a fulfilling meal, and great conversation. They go out of their way to make you feel cared for and welcome. When you stay at their home for an extended period of time, they are the ones that make you feel like their home is your home.

"Help yourself to whatever you need," they may say. A good host thinks of even the small things in taking care of your every need.

Or maybe that person is you! Perhaps you are the hostess with the most-est!

Being on the giving or receiving end of good hospitality is a special thing. Good hosts serve others well, pour into their guests, and do their best to meet their needs and then some. Guests feel good when they leave and go on their way, maybe even better than when they arrived.

A good host wouldn't invite you over to share in a meal and then limit the amount of food you could eat. When you say that you are hungry or thirsty, a good host would provide you with a snack or glass of water, not deny you food and drink or tell you to wait until the next morning to eat. They wouldn't present you with a plate of brownies and tell you that you may have only one or none. Or worse, that you better exercise after eating dessert!

Who would want to visit this person? You would feel worse after visiting them, not better as you left and went on your way.

Yet, how often do we practice good hospitality with our own bodies? How often do we ignore our body's needs? How often do we ignore it when it's hungry? How often do we deny it what it really wants? How often are we punishing ourselves for food choices with exercise?

In the Bible, John praises Gaius for the great hospitality that he shows his fellow brethren, even those that are strangers to him. In 3 John 6 he tells Gaius,

> *Please send them on their way in a manner that honors God.*

And in 3 John 8,

> *We ought therefore to show hospitality to such people so that we may work together for the truth.*

Beloved, throughout the day today, practice hospitality with yourself and send your body on its way in a manner that honors God by meeting its needs and not denying or punishing it.

Dear Gracious Father, please help us to treat our bodies as we do our guests. Help us to remember that there is no punishment for those in Christ and therefore we may live in freedom. We anticipate the mighty things you have planned for those on the healing path with food, fitness, and body image. Amen.

DAY 10: FINDING CONTENTMENT

If only I were _____ (thinner, curvier, shorter, taller, fill in the blank), then I would have_____ (love, affection, attention, approval, etc.).

Sound familiar?

It feels like changing your body would fix everything. If that were true, then super models would be the happiest people on earth. They aren't. In fact, those in the industry report that super models are some of the most body-conscious, unhappy folks around.

It's all an illusion. Having a body that society deems beautiful doesn't actually bring the happiness that is promised.

For some people, making small, gradual, sustainable changes that promote overall well-being results in changes in their body shape and size. And for others who practice these same patterns, they experience no noticeable physical changes. What's the deal? The deal is that God is a creative genius who intentionally made us all different.

What happens to your body when you treat it well depends largely on something you have no control over – your genetics.

So, you have two choices: Door A – spend hours at the gym and starve yourself, only to lose weight and gain disordered eating patterns, or door B – pursue more enjoyable, sustainable self-care practices and accept the body that results.

Door B sounds pretty appealing. Body acceptance – easier said than done, right? But certainly a goal that the Lord may be calling you to pursue.

In the letter to the Philippians, Paul encourages finding contentment with whatever you have. In his case he was discovering how to have contentment while in prison, of all places:

> *Not that I was ever in need, for I have learned how to be content with whatever I have. (Philippians 4:11)*

Finding contentment in your not-so-super-model body might feel like wishful thinking. But it's entirely possible. In fact, with God's help, it's probable.

Discover body contentment by asking God to change your thoughts. Fix your eyes on Him and ask Him to show you the amazing creation that you are.

As a society, our definition of beauty has been shaped by the media. We don't have to allow the media to define beauty. God decides what's beautiful, not the media, and He declares that you are fearfully and wonderfully made.

Dear Lord, help us to discover contentment with our bodies. Help us to see our bodies as masterpieces You have created, instead of something that needs fixing or adjusting. Help us to reject the definition of beauty fed to us by the media and replace it with the defining words you gave us in scripture. Amen.

DAY 11: LESSONS FROM A TODDLER

Children who grow up in positive, loving households are completely confident in their parents' love. They know that they can make mistakes, wear mis-matched clothes, and "let loose" a little and they will still be loved.

Consider how many days you may have woken up, looked in the mirror and criticized your body, wondering if you were loveable.

"If only my hips were slimmer. Wait. Is that cellulite on my legs? I need to work out. Look at my flabby arms! I need to get back on a diet."

How often do we judge ourselves unworthy of God's love because of either outward or inward flaws? I John 3:1 says,

> *See what great love the Father has lavished on us, that we should be called the children of God!*

If God loves us as a perfect Father, and we are His children, then we can know that we are also able to come to Him with complete confidence in His love at all times.
When we have this kind of confidence in God's love for us, it is from this place that we are slowly able to develop confidence in who we are.

Toddlers don't give a single thought to what other people think of them, nor do they compare themselves to others. As long as a loving parent is around, they are content.

In this day and age of social media and a plethora of messages from those around us telling us what we are supposed to look like, eat like, and act like, it is easy to lose our focus and begin to try to find our identity and self-worth in outward appearances.

And the more we try to conform to what society says we should be like or look like, the more we will find that we will never be good enough or worthy enough. But the beautiful truth is that Father God declared you VERY good and worthy of His unending love the moment He made you. In Genesis 1:31, we read,

God saw all that he had made, and it was very good.

In fact, you are declared just a little lower than the angels (Hebrews 2:7). He fashioned you intentionally and perfectly, and as a good Father, He loves you unconditionally.

When we meditate on this truth and allow it to seep into the very core of who we are, this is the starting point from which we can begin to accept ourselves and enjoy the body and the life that God has given us.

In this moment, no matter how we feel, no matter what we've done or haven't done, let us reach our arms up to our loving Father and say, "Pick me up?" Let Him lavish his love upon you today and know that you are beautiful in His eyes.

Dear God, thank you for loving us. May awareness of your love quiet our striving hearts today as we rest in Your arms. Amen.

DAY 12: COMPARISON

The great Theodore Roosevelt once said, "Comparison is the thief of joy." And isn't that the truth? It only takes a moment on social media for those wishes, wants, and desires to rear their ugly head. And when they do, joy flies right out the window.

The grass *always* looks very green in the lives of our friends.

We know in our hearts that it's often only the happy moments, triumphs, and good-hair-days that get posted to social media. We tell ourselves repeatedly that there's always more going on in someone's life than what we see on social media. But, despite our best efforts, the longing for what our friends have persists.

A new car

An exotic vacation

A happy marriage

Children

Singlehood

Muscles

Curves

You name it – whatever that person has that we don't have? That's what we crave.

The claws of comparison came long before social media. In fact, the sin of comparison weaves through many stories in the Bible – Cain and Able, Joseph's brothers, even the disciples who walked the earth with Jesus!

In his second letter to the Corinthians, the apostle Paul warns about comparison (10:12).

> *We do not dare to classify or compare ourselves with some who commend themselves. When they measure themselves by themselves and compare themselves with themselves, they are not wise.*

Is comparison robbing you of joy? Swim in your own lane, run your own race, and focus on the tasks God has set before you. Pursue His will in your life and celebrate His many gifts.

Maybe you don't have a new car, but if you have a way to get to work, that's something to celebrate! Your body may look nothing like your sister's body. But praise God that He made us all different! If time spent on social media triggers thoughts of comparison, perhaps this is a call to spend your time differently.

Beloved, when you do the comparison game, you question the purpose for which our heavenly Father has made you. When you were in your mama's womb, your divine reason for being born was already known. When you do the comparison game, you delete that purpose and thus never feel complete trying to be someone else. Be yourself, everyone else is taken.

Heavenly Father, protect us from the claws of comparison. Guide our thoughts to those of praises of blessings. Show us the way to contentment, leaning into Your path and purpose in our lives. Amen.

MIND

DAY 13: THE POWER OF POSITIVE THINKING

The average person thinks 50-70,000 thoughts a day. That's one busy brain. At times it feels like the mind can go in a million directions all on its own.

In a weight-obsessed culture like this one, we're bombarded with images all day long that suggest health and happiness is limited to a certain body type. It's easy for that message to shape our thoughts and actions...and not in a good way.

Negative thoughts can easily take over:
"I wish I looked like that."
"Why can't my ___ look like that?"
"I ate too much. I have no self-control."
"I'm so lazy."

Here's the good news. We have control over our thoughts. In his letter to the Philippians (4:8), Paul suggests we think differently.

> *Finally, beloved, whatever is true, whatever is honorable, whatever is just, whatever is pure, whatever is pleasing, whatever is commendable, if there is any excellence and if there is anything worthy of praise, think about these things.*

When our thoughts start from "God is love" and "God created me, therefore I am beautiful," it is much easier to choose to treat our bodies with compassion.

Do you see the difference from our thoughts starting here, instead of starting with "I am not worthy of love until I am a size_____" or "I am not lovable because I didn't follow _____ dieting rule"?

Attend to your thoughts. They determine your actions. Be mindful of the messages you tell yourself. Paul knew the power of positive thinking. When our thoughts are focused on loving ourselves because we are God's creation, our actions will be based on self-love, compassion, and grace. These are the loving thoughts that are honoring, pure, pleasing and reflective of God's Love. These thoughts spur us into action of gentle and loving food choices and joyful movement.

When we start with LOVE as our root, instead of guilt and shame, we can branch out into actions of freedom around food and exercise. Ask God to guide your thoughts towards those that are honorable, pure, and worthy of praise.

Dear God, thank You for your Spirit that helps guide our thoughts. Give us the strength and endurance to confront the thoughts that are punishing and not pure and to re-direct them to pleasing and honorable thoughts. Thank you for the gift of our bodies and our minds to help guide us in our thoughts and actions that reflect Your Love. Amen.

DAY 14: SURVIVIAL GUIDE FOR A BAD BODY DAY

Think back to your last "bad body day". You woke up, took a good hard look in the mirror, and nothing looked right, fit right, or felt right. And then there was the extra wrinkle line and gray hair that sent you right on over the edge. It wasn't a good-news day. It wasn't a day for selfies. It was a day for hiding - preferably under a mask if you could. Instead you settled for a looser fitting top, sunglasses, and a hat...a day for going incognito.

And if you take a good hard look inside yourself on those bad body days, you may notice that they have little to do with your body. Here's the truth - it's not possible that your body ACTUALLY changed while sleeping those eight hours. Think about it. All you did was sleep.

Then why on earth do you feel so rotten about yourself right here and right now?

Any therapist will tell you that a "bad body day" has little to do with your body and a whole lot to do with other stressors in your life. It's just sometimes easier to hate your body than to deal with hurt feelings, grief, a broken heart, or anger towards a partner, friend, or family member. In a study of 300 women, those who were unsatisfied with their career or relationship reported more negative body thoughts than those who were content in those areas.

So, next time the negative body talk escalates, ask yourself this:

"If this wasn't about my body, what could it be about?"

In other words, if your body wasn't the issue (pretend you were actually feeling ok about your body that day), what else might be bothering you? If it's not crystal clear, ask for God's help to discern the root cause - the real hurt and pain that might be to blame for the negative body thoughts.

The Psalmist invites God to,

> Search me, and know my heart,
> Test me and know my anxious thoughts (Psalm 139:23)

Ask God to find out what's really bothering you, and to reveal it to you. Beloved, don't be afraid of the hurt and the pain. He will carry the burden with you. He will walk you through to the other side, where you'll find peace and healing. You don't have to go it alone.

Dear God, please search me and know my heart. On those days when it feels harder to love my body, help me to uncover the other hurts and pains that I might be avoiding. Walk with me through those negative feelings and hold me in Your everlasting and loving arms. Amen.

DAY 15: THE KNEE-JERK PRAYER

In one study, women reported experiencing an average of 13 negative thoughts about their body in a given day. It's nice to know you're not alone, right? But this is no way to live. Sometimes these negative thoughts come and go, and other times they fester and spill over into relationships, careers, and home life.

God gave us the most amazing tool to fight back against these negative thoughts. He gave us prayer. With practice, a negative body thought can be countered with a prayer.

Prayers don't need to be sorted into certain parts of the day. While there's nothing wrong with a morning prayer, a bedtime prayer, or a blessing over a meal, God wants us praying all the time. The Thessalonians were encouraged to "pray without ceasing" (Thessalonians 5:16).

In fact, every bad body thought deserves a knee-jerk prayer. Imagine how your feelings about your body might shift if you were able to remember to pray each and every time you experienced a negative feeling about your body, like a knee-jerk reaction.

In 1 Timothy 2:1, Paul feels so passionate about our prayer life that he lists it first. He says,

I urge you, first of all, to pray for all people.

Prayer isn't just something to do once in a while when we REALLY need something. It's a tool we're told to visit over and over again, all day long.

So, what is the right prayer for a negative body thought? Beloved, there is no right or wrong when it comes to praying. Any prayer will do. The only "wrong" prayer is not praying at all. Even just a simple, "Help! Make those thoughts stop!" will suffice. Find the words that work for you, and simply ask God to put peace in your heart about your body. The Bible even says in Romans 8:26,

> In the same way, the Spirit helps us in our weakness. We do not know what we ought to pray for, but the Spirit Himself intercedes for us through wordless groans.

We don't even have to have the right words! He's just thrilled that we're making contact. Practice those short, little prayers throughout the day as those anxious body thoughts arise. He's listening.

Dear Lord, help us to remember to pray each and every time we experience negative thoughts about our bodies. When our "gut" is experiencing wordless groans, may we come to you in prayer. We know You made us and that you don't make mistakes. We're sorry for not always appreciating your creation. Thank you for giving us a way to communicate with You. We ask right now that You show us the way to loving our bodies. And we'll remember to keep asking for body peace that passes all understanding. Amen.

DAY 16: CHANGING THE "SHOULD" TO "COULDS"

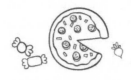

How many times have you said, "I should"? I should lose weight. I should stop eating so much sugar. I should run more. I should be more disciplined in my eating. I should... I should... I should! The thing about "shoulds" is they can lead to a place of condemnation instead of conviction. So, what's the difference?

According to the Christian Apologetics Research and Ministry, condemnation is declaring an evildoer to be guilty and can refer to the punishment inflicted on man because of that guilt. Conviction is the work of the Holy Spirit where a person is able to see himself as God sees him: guilty, defiled, and totally unable to save himself (John 16:8). Conviction in the believer brings an awareness of sin and results in repentance, confession and cleansing.

So, in laymen's terms, condemnation leads us to icky places where we often feel shamed and paralyzed to move forward. When you feel unattractive, unlovable, and helpless you may turn to food for comfort.

Conviction, on the other hand, may not feel good, but it leads to a place of redemption and moving forward. When you feel unattractive, unlovable, and helpless, you may pause to pray about next steps to take care of your physical and emotional needs. See the difference? It's subtle, but also a complete game-changer.

So very often those "shoulds" are a form of condemnation. It might be tempting to use exercise as a form of punishment for eating a pleasurable food. Be on alert dear friend, because the enemy will use shoulds to paralyze you in diets, arduous exercise routines, and body hate.

So what if we changed our "shoulds" into "coulds"...

- Could I try a different form of movement that might be more lasting?
- Could I try to add fresh colorful veggies to my plate?
- Could I try to make small changes instead of drastic ones?

I don't know about you, but there is a sense of freedom in the "could". Take heart with Romans 8:1-2 where Paul shares the good news that,

> ...there is now no condemnation for those who are in Christ Jesus because through Christ Jesus the law of the Spirit who gives life has set you FREE from the law of sin and death.

When you question whether or not the enemy is scheming to keep you chained to an unhealthy relationship with food, movement and body, ask yourself if what you are experiencing is condemnation or conviction.

Dear Heavenly Gracious Father, Satan has come to steal, kill and destroy whereas you have come to give us life and have it to the full. Allow us to see when condemnation is active and when conviction is spurring us on. Help us to change the shoulds into coulds and gain freedom through You, thereby moving one step closer to a healthy relationship with food and fitness. Amen.

DAY 17: STAYING ROOTED IN THE STORM

Within a few short minutes, a storm can wreak havoc on our homes, towns, and communities. Five minutes of golf-ball sized hail or a few well-placed lightning strikes can result in millions of dollars' worth of damage.

Consider the damage of a few short words:

"It looks like you've put on a few pounds."

It might be a well-meaning doctor, parent, or friend.

It doesn't really matter who it's from. A stormy moment on the receiving end of that message can cause damage to our emotional and physical health. Words like this can cut deep and straight to the core.

You may know in your heart that your body is fine just the way it is. You may have come to realize that God made our bodies in different shapes and sizes. (That's our hope, anyway!) And while God calls us to take care of ourselves, He's just fine with our genetic variations of body size…because He actually made us this way.

Here is the truth: your health is WAY MORE than a number on a scale. Your head might know this, but your heart experiences pain, nonetheless. Because that ache in our hearts to be loved and accepted for just who we are is also very real.

Painful words from others about your body can either sink in and cause immense damage or bounce off. What happens when those words hit ultimately depends on your foundation.

Rooting your body image in confidence and self-acceptance is more than just developing thick skin. Just as trees survive storms by digging their roots deep into the ground and holding on for dear life, laying our roots deep into Christ's love can protect us from the most serious storms of emotional wounding.

Digging deep into scripture, getting on your knees in prayer, surrounding yourself with encouraging believers, and making intentional efforts to remain in communication with Jesus throughout your day will keep your eyes focused in the right direction (looking up!), helping you weather the storms.

Let these words from Colossians 2:7 nourish your roots today:

> *Let your roots grow down into him, and let your lives be built on him. Then your faith will grow strong in the truth you were taught, and you will overflow with thankfulness.*

Heavenly Father, heal the wounds some of us have from unkind remarks about our bodies. We ask that you would protect us from the hurt and pain, which often comes from the people we love. Amen.

FOOD

DAY 18: EATING WORRY FREE

I'm a worrier. Anxious over the "what ifs" of life. And there are many, aren't there? From the big questions like, "Should I change jobs?" and "Will we need to move?" to the everyday questions like, "Will I have time to exercise?", "What will we eat for dinner?", and "Will I make it to work on time?"

In Matthew (25:25), Jesus encourages us to stress less.

> *"Therefore I tell you, do not worry about your life, what you will eat or drink; or about your body, what you will wear. Is not life more than food, and the body more than clothes?"*

Elsewhere in the Bible, we are commanded, "Do not be anxious about anything" (Phil 4:6). But here in Matthew, Jesus is specifically addressing the daily anxieties we all face and He uses the examples of food and drink. These are some of our most basic needs for survival.

In Jesus's day, when your crop yield was determined by the cooperation of weather and the absence of pests, the question of whether or not you could provide enough food for your family would likely have been paramount. Today, in the affluent society we live in where grocery stores are filled with stocked shelves of beverages, dry goods, bread, dairy, meat, and produce of every kind, you would think there's less to worry about.

Not true. Just as in biblical days, some struggle to make ends meet and get food on the table. For others, there's a whole new type of worry – anxiety about food, health, and body image.

Vegetarian, vegan, sugar free, organic, grass-fed, paleo, gluten free, dairy free, Whole30, low carb, clean eating. We are constantly being told what we should and should not eat. We are constantly being taught to fear. We fear fat so we buy lean ground beef. We fear GMOs, artificial sweeteners, food dyes, and pesticides. We fear that the foods we eat will cause chronic illness or lead to weight gain.

With all the messages about "good" foods, "bad" foods, "good" diets, and "bad" diets, it's no wonder we're anxious! Stop the press - your chicken is not free-range, and your broccoli is not organic?!

Think about all of the food and drink worries that you have in this moment. Now, listen to the words of Jesus from Matthew 6:25.

> *"Do not worry about your life, what you will eat or drink… Is not life more than food?"*

Let these words wash over your anxious spirit. His last question there is a rhetorical question. Yes, of course! Life is more than food! Jesus has come to give us an abundant, grace-filled, joyful life.

No matter where you fall on your journey to healing your relationship with food or health in general, this truth stands over all. Ultimately, no matter what we eat and drink, our lives are in the hands of a loving God who has a good plan and purpose for us. It is in this, we rest.

Heavenly Father, forgive us for spending so much time worrying about what we eat and drink that it consumes us and we forget to rest in Your loving care. Today, help us as we navigate the voices of the world around us to listen to Your voice above all. Amen.

DAY 19: FOOD AND FELLOWSHIP

If food wasn't meant to be enjoyed, then I don't think it would have been talked about so much in the Bible. Acts 2:46 reads,

> *Every day they continued to meet together in the temple courts. They broke bread in their homes and ate together with glad and sincere hearts.*

In many stories, we see people gathering together and sharing meals, not with feelings of anxiety or fearfulness about the food they were about to eat, but with *glad and sincere hearts.* The most famous of these meals was "The Last Supper" where Jesus said,

> *Take and eat; this is my body. (Matthew 26:26)*

and

> *This is my blood of the covenant, which is poured out for many for the forgiveness of sins. (Matthew 26:28)*

Yes, the emblems of communion are significant, and Jesus certainly knew what he was doing in choosing a mealtime to make a point and food and drink as a reminder of His sacrifice on the cross.

God provides food for our enjoyment and nourishment for our body and soul. Yet we feel the need to obsess about what to eat. Instead, let's take a deep breath before we sit down to eat. Take a moment to enjoy the people around you and celebrate the meal.

Let's give thanks to the Lord for providing food and a table where it can be enjoyed. Allow yourself to be slow and mindful, paying attention to tastes of foods, the temperature, the texture and truly savor the entire experience. Listen to the people you're with, taking genuine interest in what they share.

Approach the table like this today and eat as if it is The Last Supper with a close friend.

Dear God, change our hearts and minds. Take our focus off what the food will do to us and instead help us focus on the precious gift of eating. Help us enjoy food without feeling guilty, and instead focus on loving the other people at our table just as you would. Amen.

DAY 20: FOOD RULES ARE MADE TO BE BROKEN

Rules can be exhausting. From a young age we are told, "do this…don't do that." As a child, rules helped us learn. We learned to use "please" and "thank you", how to hold our forks, and even rules about bedtime. As a child, some rules were terrible! An adult-imposed naptime meant missing out on something fun! (How ironic that now as adults we'd do anything for a nap.)

As children, rules felt big and punishing. As adults, we learn from experiences God gives us and we learn what feels good in our bodies. Then why, oh why, as adults, do we insist on creating more rules?

"Eat this, don't eat that."

"Exercise at least an hour most days of the week."

"Don't eat after 6pm."

We insist on following these rules (some of which aren't even based on scientific research!) rather than learning from our God-given experiences and the body God has given us.

Paul tells us that Jesus didn't come to give us more rules. He came to set us free. The Spirit of God is often expressed with the idea of freedom in mind, apart from the law. In fact, Romans 8:1-4 says,

> *Therefore, there is now no condemnation for those who are in Christ Jesus, because*
> *through Christ Jesus the law of the Spirit who gives life has set you free from the law of sin and death.*

This idea is reiterated in 2 Corinthians 3:17:

> *Now the Lord is the Spirit, and where the Spirit of the Lord is, there is freedom.*

So, if Christ's Spirit is living in us, we are called to live into this freedom and not be bound by slavery. Oh praise, Jesus!

Freedom rings from book-to-book and chapter-to-chapter in the New Testament. My friends, lean into this truth: Food rules are self-inflicted laws. They are not from the Spirit.

Sure, we are invited to treat our bodies as living sacrifices, holy and pleasing, but how we treat our bodies isn't rule-based. This frees us up to discover which foods feel best in our bodies, and in what amounts.

Living a life without self-inflicted dieting rules means we get to move our bodies in ways and in amounts that feel best for each of us. By living in a culture that has set up diet rules, we are living counter to freedom.

We cannot be free when tethered to diet rules that require punishment or sacrifices for breaking these arbitrary food rules, such as restriction or stressful exercise. That is the kind of slavery Jesus came to abolish. You're invited to live a free and abundant life in Christ!

Dear Lord, we praise you for the freedom you gave us. Now give us the courage to break free from food rules and to trust our body's signals and your wisdom to guide our eating choices. Amen.

DAY 21: A GOD'S EYE VIEW

It's easy to lose sight of the big picture and get lost in the minute decisions that riddle our days and weeks.

We often make decisions in order to soothe or gratify in the "here and now" without thinking about the big picture.

- A food choice made to soothe an anxious heart
- A child quieted with a candy bar at the grocery store
- A weight loss plan that promises a quick fix
- A daily trip to a local coffee shop for a $4 drink when funds are tight

We are a society of instant gratification. We'd rather have it now and be in debt than wait, plan, and save.

We see what's right in front of our face, and that's about it.

Fortunately, God sees the big picture, and He has big plans for us, plans for healing, loving, and serving. Each day He is working on our hearts, chipping away at healing them as we come to Him and ask for it.

You *want* to no longer worry about every morsel you eat.

You *want* to wake up the next day free from body hate.

You *want* to stop feeling guilty about eating a cupcake…by tomorrow, at the latest.

God wants that too. But finding healing in your relationship with food and your body doesn't usually happen overnight.

You may not feel His healing presence every moment of every day, but He is at work. His timing is unique for each of us. For some, healing can be a LOOOOOOOONG, SLOOOOOOOOW process. And for others, it might take the form of an instant miracle.

Either way, He's not the sort of God who hears our cries and hands us a lollipop to make it all better. God works in *His* time. That's hard for us instant-gratification-lovers.

Be patient. Surrender to His timing and the personal growth and strength that arises from waiting. Let these words in Hebrews (12:11) soak in:

> *Now, discipline always seems painful rather than pleasant at the time, but later it yields the peaceful fruit of righteousness to those who have been trained by it.*

Beloved, peaceful fruit is headed your way.

Remember, our vision is limited, but His vision is eternal. He can see the big picture, so ask, "Be Thou My Vision" and hold out for the greater prize – His ultimate healing power, which will come at just the right time.

God, we surrender our healing journey over to you. As we wait, we will continue to sit at your feet, seeking your gentle touch on our hearts. We ask that you change us from the inside out and that you show us glimpses of your big picture vision for our lives. We will worship while we wait. Amen.

DAY 22: PERMISSIABLE? YES. BENEFICIAL? NO.

God loves us so much that He gave us free will - the freedom to live our lives built on choices we make. Therefore, we do have the freedom to jump on the next weight loss program that falls in our lap. However, the research shows that dieting isn't necessarily good for us. The on-and-off, up-and-down trends commonly seen with weight loss plans can take a toll on physical and emotional health and well-being.

And let us remember that although we have free will, our life manual called the Bible encourages us to,

> *...not turn aside from any of the commands I [Moses] give you today, to the right or to the left, following other gods and serving them. (Deuteronomy 28:14)*

We want to do the right thing. We want to obey God. However, nowhere in the Bible does it say, "Thou shalt lose weight." And nowhere in the Bible does it say, "Thou shalt not try to lose weight." There aren't any clear-cut instructions.

However, what is allowed and permitted isn't always beneficial. And in this case, the Lord is concerned most about our hearts. He wants us all in. There are certainly Biblical references to taking care of oneself and many passages warning believers about idolatry and obsessions over earthly things.

Since there are no hard and fast rules pertaining to concerns about body weight outlined in the Bible, we must look at what might be most beneficial. Paul sums this up perfectly in 1 Corinthians 10:23 when he says,

"I have the right to do anything," you say — but not everything is beneficial. "I have the right to do anything" — but not everything is constructive.

Study after study tells us that diets don't work and aren't beneficial. They can even be harmful. The good news is that we can still reap the health benefits of eating balanced meals and participating in joyful physical movement even when the scale doesn't budge.

Beloved, is God calling you to discover a gentler way to take care of yourself? Free of worries over the scale and instead filled with self-compassion, balanced, regular eating, and gentler forms of self-care? While there may not be explicit directions in the Bible for just how to do this, the Holy Spirit can guide you on your path.

Dear Lord, we praise you for the freedom of choice. Please help us to make choices that grow Your kingdom. We ask you for the courage to move away from dieting. Show us the way to lifestyle patterns that are flexible, health-enhancing, and honoring to you. Amen.

DAY 23: BREAKING BREAD TOGETHER

Jesus is facing his death on the cross, and how does he choose to spend his last few precious hours? Eating, of course! Jesus and the disciples break bread together. And yet, somehow we forget to celebrate Him when we feast.

We are all guilty of scarfing down a meal and jugging down a beverage while rushing to the next meeting, event, or workday. Food is often an afterthought. Something to be hurried or squeezed into a busy day. And, for many, food is used to cope or soothe a fear.

Food isn't meant to be obsessed over, feared, or rushed. Food is supposed to be celebrated, cherished, and savored.

Despite cultural differences worldwide, one thing is the same – food remains at the center of community and family gatherings. This was true 2,000 years ago, and holds true today. Breaking bread together is central to building community.

In fact, even as far back as Genesis, stories of food provision are woven throughout the Old and New Testaments. Genesis 1:29-30 reads,

> *Then God said, "I give you every seed-bearing plant on the face of the whole earth and every tree that has fruit with seed in it. They will be yours for food. And to all the beasts of the earth and all the birds in the sky and all the creatures that move along the ground — everything that has the breath of life in it — I give every green plant for food." And it was so.*

In the Old Testament, the Lord provided manna and later in the New Testament, feasting was central to Jesus's teaching, service, and miracles. It's one way he loved others. He made loaves and fishes multiply to feed a hungry audience. He made it so that fisherman could cast nets and weigh down their boats with an abundance; and in his final hours, Jesus used food to remind us of His sacrifice on the cross in the name of His everlasting love for us.

In the hands of the enemy, food can be devastating to health, body image, and self-worth. However, when we use food as a central means to nourish, enjoy, and commune, it glorifies God.

Heavenly Father, we praise you for giving us the pleasure of eating. Thank you for showing us that food is meant to be honored, celebrated, and appreciated. Help us to remember to experience food how you meant for us to experience it – together and with thankful hearts. Amen.

TOOLS FOR VICTORY

DAY 24: WILLPOWER? OR GOD'S WILL?

Dieters are often very evangelistic about their eating plan. They want everyone to do it with them. They share a list of dos and don'ts like it's gospel.

There's something intriguing and maybe even enticing about a new diet. While no one likes rules, we are certainly captivated by the thought of being in control. So much in life feels out of control – a job, a loved one, children. At times, controlling food and following a clear-cut set of rules is tempting, especially if the testimonials and promises of the dieting marketers are on point.

Any dieter can tell you that weight loss regimens require willpower. Willpower is defined as, "control exerted to do something or restrain impulses."

Dieters try to create rules and regulations to achieve an "ideal" or "perfect" body but the rules are rarely sustainable. They usually result in feelings of deprivation, hunger, and irritability in the long run. Then dieters blame themselves for ultimately falling off their plan saying, "If I only had more willpower."

Truth be told, it's not willpower that you need. It's God's power that conquers all. And God may not actually be calling you to a restrictive new dieting plan. In fact, He's probably not. He knows that a new diet plan won't lead to abundant living. God knows that there's no place for calorie-counting and illusions of control when He is the one who is in control.

In Colossians 2, Paul confronts false teachings that objected to eating and drinking for enjoyment. At the time, folks weren't dieting to change their bodies, but participating in restrictive practices for religious reasons. He explains that these rules were based on human commands and teachings (and not from Jesus).

> *Such regulations indeed have an appearance of wisdom, with their self-imposed worship, their false humility and their harsh treatment of the body, but they lack any value in restraining sensual indulgence. (Colossians 2:23)*

Beloved, only Jesus can tell you how to live your life. God gave you one body with perfect signals to guide you in your eating decisions. He also gave you a wide range of food flavors, colors and textures that are to be celebrated. Food is meant to be joyful and a source of pleasure. Celebrate these gifts and ask for God's will (instead of willpower) and direction in taking care of the body He gave you.

Dear God, thank you for showing us that it's Your will that we need and crave in how we live our lives. May we not be tempted by diets, with their illusions of control, and instead turn to you for the way, the truth, and the light. Amen.

DAY 25: THE HAMSTER WHEEL

Life feels like a hamster wheel at times. Our days are filled with business and scurrying, but we're getting nowhere. Running off to work, studying for classes, planning a party, taking kids to some kind of practice, or taking care of an aging parent...all while scarfing down food or skipping meals just to try and keep up. No matter what your hamster wheel looks like, do you ever long for rest?

One thing we repeatedly see throughout Jesus's life (played out in the gospels, Matthew, Mark, Luke, and John) is the value of rest. Jesus is being called to work miracles left and right, but he sets clear boundaries in order to spend more time in solitude and prayer.
Mark 1:35 is just one of many examples of Jesus being intentional about finding solitude:

> *Very early in the morning, while it was still dark, Jesus got up, left the house and went off to a solitary place, where he prayed.*

Jesus needs to escape from the crowds to desolate places to recharge. After running all day, trying to meet both the expectations of others and the expectations we place on ourselves, we need to escape to a desolate mountain top where we can pause, breathe, think, pray, and just be. In Matthew 11:28, Jesus says,

> *Come to me, all who labor and are heavy laden, and I will give you rest.*

The rest that Jesus gives is not something we achieve, but something we *receive*. He came to this earth as God in human flesh, conquering sin and death on the cross, so that He could carry our burdens for us and give us true life-restoring, rejuvenating rest.

There are many ways to care for our bodies – nourishing and pleasurable meals, physical activity, hydration, human connection – and don't miss this one – rest! Add rest to your list of self-care strategies.

Our bodies require a lot of TLC to function. Feeling drained or irritable? It could be so many things. Perhaps you're really just dehydrated and need a drink of water. Or maybe your energy stores are depleted and you need a hearty meal. It could be that a vigorous walk to blow off some steam is what your body is asking for. Or maybe you simply need a nap. Often the simple act of rest gets overlooked as the logical answer to our body's physical and spiritual needs.

You don't have to keep running! Stop. Lift your eyes to Jesus. He is the giver of rest.

Jesus, instead of striving to get somewhere on that hamster wheel, help me to receive the rest only You can give. I release my burdens to You. Restore my soul. Amen.

DAY 26: GIVE THANKS

Aging is inevitable. And, if you have dealt with body image issues all your life, the aging process may bring enhanced strife. You might find that your body has started to change, you need glasses, a crown on a tooth or maybe you find some pesky gray hairs.

However, with age grows wisdom. The obvious wisdom comes from the truth that Jesus is our joy, not perfect teeth, not perfect eyes and not fitting in jeans that you wore at 20. Praise the Lord that our identity is in Him. He shows us that through His joy he brings such rich moments in life. This gift is a choice you can give yourself – the gift of gratitude.

Gratitude is defined as the quality of being thankful; readiness to show appreciation for and to return kindness. Research shows that those who choose gratitude, versus focusing on the negative, feel better about their lives and are healthier.

And even more powerful are the words of Paul in the New Testament. He reminds us in Philippians 4:6-7:

> *Don't be anxious about anything; rather, bring up all your requests to God in your prayers and petitions, along with giving thanks. Then the peace of God that exceeds all understanding will keep your hearts and minds safe in Christ Jesus.*

Although we cannot change the aging process, we can change our attitude about it. Although we can make changes in our eating and activity patterns, we don't have control over what happens to our body shape or size. Instead of changing your outer appearance, why not try an attitude of gratitude?!

The saying, "fake it 'till you make it" applies here. You may not be experiencing authentic gratitude each and every day for your body, but on those days in particular, see if you can muster up a prayer of gratitude. The Lord your God applauds your efforts, and you'd be amazed at how by simply giving thanks your whole mindset can change.

Dear God, we come to You today asking to help us thrive in the bodies You gave us and let go of striving for more...or less. And when we find it difficult to let go of striving to be thin, more beautiful, or a different body, let us do as Paul instructed and bring that concern to You. Let us choose gratitude even when we aren't feeling so thankful. Amen.

INSPIRATION

DAY 27: COMFORTER

Ever walked with a friend through a hard time? It's hard to know what to say…to find just the right words that bring encouragement and cheer.

Here's the good news, Beloved. God's here 24/7, and he's got just the right responses to the longings of our hearts. The psalmist wrote,

> *When the cares of my heart are many, Your consolations cheer my soul. Psalms 94:19*

Our heavenly Father wants us to bring Him our troubles. Body struggles may sound like petty stuff to be bringing to the feet of Jesus, but God says, "bring it on!" He wants to replace your thoughts with His thoughts.

Your thoughts might sound like this:

I don't look good in this outfit. I need to change into something that makes me look thinner. Maybe I need to lose weight.
I wish I had curly hair, then it wouldn't look so boring.
I wish I had straight hair; it would be so much more manageable.
I need to pack a healthy lunch today. If I don't watch what I eat I'll just gain weight.
When will I have time to exercise today? I need to make it happen otherwise I'm just being lazy.

God's consolations sound like this:

1 John 4:9-10. This is how God showed his love among us: He sent his one and only Son into the world that we might live through him. This is love: not that we loved God, but that he loved us and sent his Son as an atoning sacrifice for our sins.

Genesis 1:31. And God saw everything that he had made, and behold, it was very good. And there was evening and there was morning, the sixth day.

1 Peter 5:6-7. Humble yourselves, therefore, under the mighty hand of God so that at the proper time he may exalt you, casting all your anxieties on him, because he cares for you.

Colossians 2:6-7. Therefore, as you have received Christ Jesus the Lord, so walk in Him, having been firmly rooted and now being built up in Him and established in your faith, just as you were instructed, and overflowing with gratitude.

Jeremiah 29:11. "For I know the plans I have for you," declares the LORD, "plans to prosper you and not to harm you, plans to give you hope and a future."

Beloved, ask God to meet you in your pain and show you His great love for you today. Meditate on His words to you. Refer back to this list and pray over these truths. Ask for His love to fill the space that your fears and worries are taking up. You are His Beloved; in Him find rest.

Dear God, we lift up our body struggles to you today. We praise you for the words You gave us in the Bible that console our deepest, darkest hurts. Thank you for being a 24/7 God. We pray that Your words would soothe our hurting souls. Amen.

DAY 28: ON BEING LOVELY

You are lovely. Somedays you may not feel so lovely – hair sticking up, circles under the eyes, disheveled. But Psalm 84:1 declares that the place where the Lord dwells is lovely.

How lovely is your dwelling place, Oh Lord God Almighty!

So, if you asked Jesus into your heart, then he dwells in you. Then guess what that makes you? Lovely!

Often times we think of the sanctuary of the Lord (or His dwelling place) as a temple, a building, or a set of walls we can walk into worship and hear truth. However, it would be a grave oversight to not realize that of all His dwelling places God calls lovely, you are on the top of His list.

We were created to be the manifest glory of God and He delights so much in us. He calls us lovely! James 1:25 says,

> *But whoever looks intently into the perfect law that gives freedom, and continues in it, not forgetting what they have heard, but doing it they will be blessed in what they do.*

There is blessing beyond what we can imagine in trusting the Word is God-breathed, looking intently into it, and acting as if it is really true. What would life look like if we, as the body of Christ and His bride, *really* believed we are lovely? Lovely is defined as "exquisitely beautiful!" And to the Lord, that is what you are.

When you are tempted to look at your reflection and criticize, recite these words, "How lovely is your dwelling place, Oh Lord God Almighty!" In other words, "I am exquisitely beautiful!" If the creator of everything we see, in His infinite wisdom and holiness, sees us this way, may we have the courage to trust Him and allow Him to change how we see ourselves, speak about ourselves, and ultimately how we live out our days.

Dear Lord, thank you for dwelling in us and for calling us lovely. Help us to claim that truth and see ourselves through your eyes – as exquisitely beautiful. Amen.

DAY 29: GLOW IN THE DARK

Adam and Eve ate the fruit from the tree. Thus, by default, that makes all of us sinners. Perhaps we don't even realize the many forms our sin takes – self-hatred, immense shame about what we eat, and even compulsively exercising. These habits can lead us to a very dark place that causes isolation. We may hide in the dark to try and cover our sin and allow a war to be waged with our bodies and minds.

But here is where the story changes…for the better. John 1:5 states,

> *The light shines in the darkness, and the darkness has not overcome it.*

You see friend, no matter what you do, if you are a believer in Christ, darkness will never prevail! The war was finished on the cross!

Perhaps you are at a place where every day you say, "I am going to lose weight and then I will go to the beach," "I will start working out harder so I can wear a smaller size," or "I hate looking in the mirror at my body." Many of us have been there and that is because we are all broken. Remember good ole Adam and Eve? We can thank them for our brokenness.

BUT, we can do something about it. We can take our brokenness and let the light shine through to make marvelous colors. We can go to the beach TODAY, as we are. We can experiment with different kinds of movement that brings us joy. We can wear clothes that fit us NOW instead of waiting to get to a certain size.

If you feel like a piece of broken shattered glass, let the light shine through it right where you are. The colors produced will surprise you and allow others to see the undeniable light of Christ shining through YOU.

Dear God, thank you for the Bible that helps us understand why we are sinners. Help us through our sin of body shame and distorted thoughts about food, exercise and health. Help us to believe that we truly can glow in the dark right where we are, and shine Your light in the world. Amen.

DAY 30: LOOK UP

As a culture, we are obsessed with earthly things. Clothes, shoes, jewelry, make-up, and even our own flesh and bones. – all are earthly things. They are everywhere you look. Advertisements left and right shout, "pick me!", "you need me!", "your social status depends on having me!"

Advertisers aren't totally satisfied until we are unsatisfied. See, it's impossible to sell things to folks who are content and satisfied.

On their own, earthly things aren't inherently bad. A new high tech watch might be useful and be a source of happiness as it is unwrapped from the packaging. However, earthly things can also be a source of preoccupation. Whether it's wanting a different look, a new car, or a little less cellulite – it's all wanting, and the satisfaction that comes from obtaining earthly things is always temporary. The earthly gain satisfies only until the next advertisement comes along.

In 1 Timothy (6:6-8), Paul reminds us to be content with what we have - that food and clothing are enough and that earthly things remain just that – on earth.

> But godliness with contentment is great gain. For we brought nothing into the world, and we can take nothing out of it. But if we have food and clothing, we will be content with that.

Beloved, true kingdom living, is giving thanks to God for having clothes, shoes, make-up and the very bodies He made for our souls to inhabit. It's time we stop wishing we had more or wishing that our bodies were less.

Paul says, "We can take nothing out [of this world]." Do you think when we are reunited with Jesus one day that we're going to be concerning ourselves with our appearances or weight? No way! Look up, dear one.

In his letter to the Colossians (3:2), Paul recommends we let go of our earthly wants and instead set our minds on Him in heaven above.

Set your minds on things above, not on earthly things.

Dear God, thank you for the reminder of what is important. Quiet our earthly desires so that we can keep our eyes fixed on You. Help us to remember that material objects or a new look will never satisfy. Only You can satisfy and sustain us. Amen.

FOR MORE ENCOURAGEMENT AND TRUTH

Instagram: @body_bloved

Facebook: **www.facebook.com/bodybloved/**

Website: **www.bodybloved.com**

If this devotional has helped heal your relationship with food or your body we would love to hear from you! Feel free to email us at **nicole@bodybloved.com** or write us a review on amazon.com.

Looking for some individual support with food struggles? We're here to help! Body Bloved registered dietitians are followers of Jesus and highly trained nutrition experts. We can help you improve your health in a variety of ways including your eating habits and patterns, nutrition related health problems, physical activity, and your relationship with food and your body.

As Christians, we can tailor our nutrition services from a Christian perspective. We are not experts in theology and we do not have a Bible degree, but we do have confidence and faith in what the Lord says to us about food and our bodies.

You can find more information at **www.bodybloved.com/faith-based-nutrition-counseling**

Thanks so much for reading!

Made in USA - Kendallville, IN
1115232_9781705539514
05.26.2020 0803